GOD, MONEY &
YOU

GOD, MONEY &
YOU

ROBERT F. COX

Copyright © 2020 by Robert F. Cox.

Library of Congress Control Number:	2020904837
ISBN: Hardcover	978-1-7960-9385-8
Softcover	978-1-7960-9384-1
eBook	978-1-7960-9383-4

All rights reserved. No part of this book may be reproduced or transmitted in any form or by any means, electronic or mechanical, including photocopying, recording, or by any information storage and retrieval system, without permission in writing from the copyright owner.

The views expressed in this work are solely those of the author and do not necessarily reflect the views of the publisher, and the publisher hereby disclaims any responsibility for them.

Scripture quotations marked KJV are from the Holy Bible, King James Version (Authorized Version). First published in 1611. Quoted from the KJV Classic Reference Bible, Copyright © 1983 by The Zondervan Corporation.

Any people depicted in stock imagery provided by Getty Images are models, and such images are being used for illustrative purposes only.
Certain stock imagery © Getty Images.

Print information available on the last page.

Rev. date: 03/11/2020

To order additional copies of this book, contact:
Xlibris
1-888-795-4274
www.Xlibris.com
Orders@Xlibris.com
811009

CONTENTS

Dedication vii
Introduction ix

Chapter 1 What Are Money & Wealth? 1
Chapter 2 Misquoted Scriptures & Stories 5
Chapter 3 Examples of Money & Wealth 15
Chapter 4 God's Purpose for Money & Wealth 25
Chapter 5 Make Money Work for You 35
Chapter 6 God is a God of Increase 43
Chapter 7 As You Think 49
Chapter 8 Prosperity Preaching 53
Chapter 9 Loans & Credit Cards 59

Conclusion 67

Dedication

My wife Cynthia was the one person who always believed in my ideas giving me her full support in all that I did. She passed away on February 21, 2019, but she knew that I had begun to write a book on the subject of money and wealth. This book is actually the result of our many hours of discussion about the topic of money and wealth. Our talks led the two of us to search the bible for scriptures referencing money and wealth which caused us to wonder why we and other Christians were struggling so much financially. I dedicate this book to my wife Cynthia because she always believed that God's people were not meant to be poor but wealthy servants doing the heavenly Father's will on the earth.

Introduction

I have listened for many years as Christians have debated the topic of money and whether or not the followers of Christ are to be wealthy or rich. In my beginning years as a saved person I was taught or led to believe that having money was evil and wrong. Then as I grew in my walk and relationship with Jesus, I began to seriously study the idea of having wealth or money in the scriptures. Through the course of repeatedly studying the word of God. I realized that having money and wealth is not offensive to God, rather it is a part of His plan for the lives of His people if they would only stop believing lies and misquoting scripture. The bible is not just a book about having faith in God and living right it is also a manual for financial success if one were to really study the scriptures. There are great truths about how to make the most out of life, unfortunately many bible readers never learn or unlock these principles so that they can apply them to their lives. If you are a believer who feels that God does not like wealthy people or money then I would encourage you to open your mind to the possibility that you could be wrong. Allow the heavenly Father to open your mind and understanding to the real financial gems that are contained within the greatest book ever written. In doing so you will no longer be blind to what God has to say about money and wealth which will allow you to go after and to have a better quality of life than you may be currently experiencing. The devil has kept you in the dark long enough about money or wealth by convincing you that it is evil and now is the time for you to receive new revelation about how money and wealth should be used in your life. I know you may be a bit nervous or skeptical about what I am saying to you but I was once the same way until I learned God's perspective on the issue. Having learned God's truths on money and wealth has set me free from wrong thinking. A new door has been opened which allows me to seek financial opportunities that will generate wealth which I can use for my own personal enjoyment along with helping to finance the work of God's kingdom. No longer do I look at wealthy people with anger or rage. My perspective has changed and now I think to myself and wonder how did they achieve their financial success and what do they do with their money and wealth. Money is something that everyone needs so that they can pay their financial obligations whether it's a mortgage, car note, student loans, utilities, medical bills or some other expense that they have incurred. Solomon writes in *Ecclessiates 10:19 (KJV) A feast is made for laughter, and wine maketh merry: but money answereth all things.* This is a powerful and true statement about money because we all need it to take care of our obligations. God cannot bless you with ideas that will generate money and wealth in your life until your thinking changes. He is waiting for you to adjust your mindset and see things differently then God will begin to give you ideas that are designed for you to prosper. It is my hope that as you read this book that you will have the things that hinder you about money and wealth. Fall off of you so that you can move into a new level of financial blessings. Let us begin our journey into the pages of this book to transform your future.

Chapter One

What Are Money & Wealth?

*But my God shall supply all your need according to
his riches in glory by Christ Jesus.
Philippians 4:19 (KJV)*

As we begin this first chapter of the book let us consider for just a moment the thought, what is money because we need to understand what exactly is considered money. A definition of money would be that it is a medium of exchange in the form of coins and banknotes that can be used to purchase goods and services. The currency of some countries has more value than others so it is important to obtain currency that has a greater value. Now that we have a definition for money we now need one for wealth which is the assets, property and resources owned by someone or something. Just from looking at the definition of wealth we can immediately see why owning a house or land is important for building wealth. Many people work extremely hard for their money and often spend their income loosely which results in them not having enough of it to save for a rainy day. People like to spend large amounts of their money on nice new and shiny things like cars, jewelry, cell phones, designer clothes, fancy dinners and expensive vacations. There is nothing wrong with someone buying new and expensive items if they can afford to do so. However, most people purchase expensive items that cause them to become overextended financially which leads to stress and poverty over a period of time. Money has great power to bless or to curse our lives depending on how we use it so we need to be smart and wise with the money that we receive. I was an avid reader of a business magazine that talked constantly about homeownership and using it to build wealth and as a homeowner I now understand why this publication stressed that point. When someone has a home that person can use the property as an investment and build equity that can be used by the homeowner. Some people use the equity in their houses to pay for college for their children and others use it to pay off or down debts and other things. Everyone needs money because without it you cannot purchase food or the other daily necessities yet some believers feel strongly that money is bad and hated by God. One of the statements I often make to fellow Christians about money being evil is for them to go to the grocery store and when they are finished shopping. Get in line to pay for their items and after the cashier rings up all of the food items tell the cashier that Jesus paid it all. Now of course I am joking about actually doing this but my point to my brothers and sisters in Christ who have a problem with money is that they need money like all people do. The cashier will be waiting for the person to pay by either cash, check or a credit card for what was in the shopping cart.

Money is not evil, good or bad it is just coins and currency a medium of exchange that people may do bad things to obtain it. Once a person understands thoroughly that money is not good or bad that it is just simply something to be used to purchase goods and services. Then I believe that person has opened the door of their heart to be transformed in how they think about money and wealth. There must be a transformation that takes places so that someone can begin to see and understand how God views money and wealth from a biblical perspective. I remember as a child in church hearing preachers speak of the ills of having money and watching how the congregation would agree. The people agreed because they were taught to hate money and wealth because traditionally ministers spoke about God having a dislike for money and wealth. It was a widely held belief among many

Christians that money and wealth would pull you off course and away from serving God so it was better to be needy or broke. I never really understood this point of view and after becoming a Christian there were many fellow believers who would tell me of this long held tradition of having little or no money as being godly. For a time I fell victim to this unscriptural idea and even briefly considered a vow of poverty because I thought that would bring me closer to God. Thankfully it was only a thought and I never made it a reality because it would have been destructive and it would not have strengthen or brought me closer to God. A vow of poverty would have only made me angry, confused and bitter in life and really it would have displeased God. As I think back over that idea of a vow of poverty I understand that it was really the devil's way of trying to keep me from living and experiencing the very best that God has for my life. When we lack understanding about money and wealth as believers it is the devil's way of blocking the blessings that God has for us and we need the mind of Christ to overcome these obstacles about money and wealth. The strongholds about money and wealth must be destroyed or we will never experience God's best for our lives. It is time for the followers of Christ to take back what belongs to them because they have been in lack far too long. If by chance you are experiencing financial lack in your life then you may need to examine your feelings about money and wealth. Perhaps you are holding onto the idea that money and wealth are evil or wrong for a Christian to have and this point of view must change. I pray that the Holy Spirit will come upon you in such a way that your understanding about money and wealth will change for you and your descendants.

Highlights/Notes

1. Money is a medium of exchange for purchasing goods and services.

2. Money is usually in the form of coins and currency.

3. Wealth is assets, property and resources that someone has.

4. Everyone needs money for their daily needs.

5. Money can be a blessing or curse depending on how it is used.

6. Owning a house or land can help in building wealth.

7. Money is neither evil, good nor bad.

Chapter Two

Misquoted Scriptures & Stories

*Wisdom is the principal thing; therefore get wisdom:
and with all thy getting get understanding.*
Proverbs 4:7 (KJV)

In order to change our mindset about money and wealth we first must understand how we got to a place of confusion on this subject. Which comes from years of hearing preachers and Christians misquote and take scriptures out of its intended context. It is important to correct this wrong thinking and to get wisdom and a good understanding to transform our minds to the truth about money and wealth. One of the first scriptures that I often hear people who are not saved along believers misquote is; *1 Timothy 6:10 (KJV) For the love of money is the root of all evil: which while some coveted after, they have erred from the faith, and pierced themselves through with many sorrows.* People will quickly say that money is the root of all evil which is not a correct statement because it is the love for money that drives people to do evil things. Once again I must tell you that money is neither good nor bad but what people do to obtain it is the problem. When you have people who will rob other people on the street taking another person's money or a pimp making a woman sell her body to strange men for money. Or a person who is willing to sell drugs or steal someone's identity to make a profit what this really speaks about is the evil that is in that person's heart. What drives one person to work honestly for a living while another uses dishonest methods to get money tells us the motive of a person rather than that money is evil. The sooner that we are willing to understand and acknowledge this difference will help us to change our views about money being evil and something that God dislikes. If you are consumed with the idea of getting and needing money then you will allow it to control you which will lead you to always seeing money as evil. However, if you understand that money is needed but God will supply what you need in abundance as long as the Father and His kingdom are first in your life. Then you will never have to chase after money and wealth because God will cause it to always find you.

The next scripture that is misquoted is; *Matthew 6:24 (KJV) No man can serve two masters: for either he will hate the one, and love the other; or else he will hold to the one, and despise the other. Ye cannot serve God and mammon.* This verse of scripture was spoke by Jesus when He was teaching the people about being devoted servants to God the Father. During Jesus' time mammon commonly referred to money, cattle and land. It should be obvious that when we are loyal and devoted to God that money is not our primary focus. Jesus felt that it was important to remind His followers to keep things in the right perspective by saying that material items or wealth should not be first in a person's life because when this is the case the money, material items and wealth have become that person's god. We can have money and wealth but those things are not supposed to take a hold of us and interfere with our relationship with God. Jesus wanted believers to understand that nothing and no one should be more important to us than God and our relationship with Him. Unfortunately this scripture has been used repeatedly to convince Christians that money and wealth are evil and that God hates these items. I must tell you that God does not hate money or wealth but He dislikes it when those things control our actions and lives. Christians have been saved by the sacrifice of Jesus to be led by the Holy Spirit and not by a greed or lust for money. Serving God first means that we as believers know the heavenly Father will take care of us and pour out to us in abundance what we need as far as money and wealth are concerned.

There is another story that people use in trying to prove that God is against money and wealth which is found in the Gospel of Luke *(Luke 16:19-31)*. The story is told by Jesus and involves a rich man and a poor beggar named Lazarus. In the story the rich man has a great life enjoying all of the finest things that his money and wealth can buy while Lazarus who is covered with sores lays at the rich man's gate begging for food. Lazarus is hungry and he is willing to eat the crumbs that fall from the rich man's table. What makes matters worse if that were possible for Lazarus is that the dogs are constantly licking his sores. Then one day Lazarus dies and is in heaven while the rich man has also died and he is in hell and torment. When people hear this they immediately believe that Lazarus went to heaven because he was poor while they also think that the rich man went to hell because of his money and wealth. Lazarus went to heaven because he was the type of person who despite his illness and what he lacked financially had a relationship with God. The rich man did not go to hell because of his money and wealth rather because he did not serve God and was selfish only caring for himself. He could have taken some of his money and wealth and tried to help Lazarus but he was not interested in the welfare of others. Money and wealth do not cause someone to go to heaven or hell receiving salvation through Christ or rejecting it is the determining factor where a person will spend eternity.

The thought or idea of someone being in love with their money or wealth comes from another story that is misunderstood by Christians and involves Jesus talking with a rich young ruler *(Mark 10:17-31)*. In this particular story Jesus meets a young man who has been able through his own ability to acquire a substantial amount of wealth who decides to ask Jesus what does he need to do to inherit eternal life. Jesus responds to the young man's question with one of His own about the commandments and about not committing adultery, stealing, killing, being a false witness, defrauding others and honoring his parents. This young man responds with excitement to Jesus saying that he has not broken any of the commandments in his life. His answer to Jesus' question causes the Lord to marvel at him then the young man is told to sell his wealth and give the money to the poor and then to come and follow Jesus. Surely this is not what the young man wanted to hear because he went away extremely sad after learning what he needed to do. The reason for Jesus telling the rich young man to sell his possessions was not because Jesus hates wealthy people but simply because the wealth had become god in the man's life. After the wealthy young man leaves the Lord continues His discussion on money and wealth. Two other scriptures that are used in the conversation are the same ones often used by some preachers who will try to show that God dislikes rich people. *Mark 10:24-25 (KJV) And the disciples were astonished at his words. But Jesus answereth again, and saith unto them, Children, how hard is it for them that trust in riches to enter into the kingdom of God. It is easier for a camel to go through the eye of a needle, than for a rich man to enter into the kingdom of God.* By hearing Jesus speak these two verses of scriptures caused the disciples to be shocked because people at that time assumed that rich or wealthy people were favored by God. Jesus mentioned that individuals who trust in their riches will have a hard time entering the kingdom of God. Trust in their riches is the key word because to serve God means that you trust Him and not your money or wealth. Our heavenly Father does not mind people having money or wealth but He does not want that money or wealth to become a god. Anytime that money or wealth becomes our god it has taken the heavenly Father's place in our heart and that is out of order. Oftentimes ministers will use this story of the rich young ruler as proof that God hates wealthy people and there are many misinformed believers who will agree with this wrong thinking. It is time for the body of Christ to turn away from the wrong thinking and attitude about money and wealth. Along with this story is another scripture that ties directly to this one; *Mark 8:36 (KJV) For what shall it profit a man, if he shall gain the whole world, and lose his own soul?* What a powerful question that Jesus has asked concerning those who would follow in His footsteps in ministering to the world because they would have to make some sacrifices to do God's work. However, this scripture has been used to make believers think that every rich or wealthy person has sold their soul to get what they have acquired. Once again a scripture is taken out of context and used to convince people that money and wealth are evil and hated by God. This is why it is so important for the people of God to spend time reading the bible for themselves to get a proper understanding.

The idea of God not liking money or wealth and wanting people especially His people to be poor, broke and disgusted can be further cleared up by looking at additional scriptures on this controversial topic. In the book of Proverbs we find another powerful nugget, *Proverbs 10:22 (KJV) The blessing of the Lord, it maketh rich, and he addeth no sorrow with it.* If God had a problem with money or wealth then why would He want to give blessings that make believers rich? Every time our heavenly Father blesses His people it will bring increase to their lives and does not cause them sadness. As I child when my parents would give me a gift especially if it was money that gift brought increase and joy to my life. God wants to bless His people so that they may experience increase in their lives. We can also study the scriptures and learn that God wants His people to prosper in all that they do and for them to be lenders. This is pointed out in, *Deuteronomy 28:12-13 (KJV) The Lord shall open unto thee his good treasure, the heaven to give rain unto thy land in his season, and to bless all the work of thine hand: and thou shalt lend unto many nations, and thou shalt not borrow. And the Lord shall make thee the head, and not the tail; and thou shalt be above only, and thou shalt not be beneath; if that thou hearken unto the commandments of the Lord thy God, which I command thee this day, to observe and to do them.* Reading these two verses should cause a doubter to become excited about God wanting them to have money and wealth. God is telling us that we can have money and wealth as long as we do things His way. What an eye opening revelation that God wants the best for our lives and that definitely includes money and wealth. Hopefully you now realize why it is important for you to change your mind set about money and wealth. God wants you to be the one who lends to others and in order for you to be a godly lender you need money or wealth. Money and wealth are a part of God's divine plan for believers so I encourage you to let that sink into your mind and spirit. The sooner you make that change mentally the quicker you can begin to transform your finances.

Now we must address the issue or idea of Jesus the Savior of the world being poor and broke. I have to admit that when I first received salvation I believed that Jesus was poor and broke which I thought was what made Him so powerful and holy. Little did I know at the time that I was completely wrong being deceived and many Christians have been taught that Jesus was poor and broke which is based on the story of His birth in a manger. The story of the birth of Jesus really should not confuse anyone and looking at one particular verse should make it clear that Jesus was not poor; *Luke 2:7 (KJV) And she brought forth her first-born son, and wrapped him in swaddling clothes, and laid him in a manger; because there was no room for them in the inn.* What should immediately stand out is the fact that the inn was full there were no more vacancies and when Mary's water broke the baby was on the way. Mary and Joseph had money or the ability to pay for accommodations but the place was booked. Preachers have been misusing this story for years saying the poor family could not afford to get a room so the baby could be born in a decent place which is totally wrong. They even talk about the infant Jesus being wrapped in swaddling cloth referring to it as if Mary and Joseph put the baby in a bunch of rags which is not true. During that time all babies were wrapped in swaddling clothes which was designed to help the limbs of the infant to grow straight. Mary and Joseph more than likely had these swaddling clothes with them and prepared to use them when Jesus was born. The parents of Jesus did not just gather some rags that happened to be laying on the ground near the manger and wrap the baby in them.

Another story that people overlook about the life of Jesus is that of the Wise Men who traveled a great distance to see and to worship Jesus as a young child. These men brought with them frankincense and myrrh, two expensive oils that could be sold for money along with gold a form of currency. With these items Joseph and Mary would have additional money to help them with their daily living expenses. However, many of the followers of Christ ignore this fact about the life of Jesus and continue to say that the Lord was poor and broke. The same way that the Wise Men put riches into the hands of Joseph and Mary our heavenly Father wants to do the same for each of His children today. There is another reference from scripture that people use to support the claim of a poor Jesus that comes from a statement that He made while talking to a scribe who wanted to come and follow the Lord. Jesus tells the scribe; *Matthew 8:20 (KJV) And Jesus saith unto him, The foxes have holes, and the birds of the air have nests; but the Son of man hath not where to lay his head.* Now the point that Jesus was trying to make to the scribe was this man willing to make the sacrifices that the Lord had made in traveling from city to city and town to town. Would the scribe be willing to spend long periods of time away from family and friends because fulfilling His mission required making many sacrifices in the Lord's life. Let us look at another situation where people further misquote scripture which involves the time that Jesus chased the money changers and merchants out of the Temple courtyard. The Lord did not chase them out of the courtyard because He hated their money or wealth rather he disliked the fact that they were taking advantage of the people and overcharging them. In other words Jesus does not like people who are dishonest in their business practices and this story serves as a warning to treat people fairly and not to overcharge customers. Hopefully the next time that you read this story in the bible you will look at it from a different point of view and receive greater understand. It seems that the only people who have a problem with money and wealth are the believers who are supposed to have it and this has to change.

Lastly in our discussion on Jesus and whether or not He was broke we must look at some of the disciples. Jesus was around people of different levels of wealth or income when He was in human form and some of His disciples were doing well for themselves in life. Matthew was a tax collector and those who had this occupation were considered wealthy which means that this disciple probably had made a pretty decent living for himself. Then we must look at Peter, Andrew, James and John these four men were all partners in a commercial fishing business. They were successful fishermen and as they followed and traveled with Jesus the business continued to operate in their absence. Nothing is given about the lives or occupations of the other disciples except for Judas who served as the treasurer for the disciples. It is interesting to me that if Jesus was poor and broke then why was there a treasurer because to have a treasurer means you have to have money. I know people who are poor and broke but they have never made a comment to me about having a treasurer. By now I hope that you are beginning to see Jesus in a new light and not buy into the idea or belief that the Lord was poor and broke. Remember that when Jesus was crucified at Calvary that the soldiers gambled for His clothing because He wore very nice clothing so God the Father did not allow His only begotten Son to be in lack or to dress poorly so why would our heavenly Father want you to be poor, broke and dressed shabby. Our heavenly Father wants you to look good on the outside and to feel good on the inside about yourself. I know that when I am dressed up in a nice suit I feel good about myself which helps to give me a better attitude about life. When we look our best we often want to give our best in all that we do. Give your best to God the Father on a daily basis and He will give His best at all times.

Highlights/Notes

1. God does not hate rich or wealthy people.

2. God wants to put money and wealth into your hands.

3. Jesus did not live a life of poverty.

4. Learn to see money and wealth from God's perspective.

5. Do not allow preachers to convince you that Jesus was poor.

6. Always make serving God first in your life.

7. Do not make money and wealth your god.

Chapter Three

Examples of Money & Wealth

But thou shalt remember the Lord thy God: for it is he that giveth thee power to get wealth, that he may establish his covenant which he sware unto thy fathers, as it is this day.
Deuteronomy 8:18 (KJV)

In the above scripture we learn that God gives His people the ability to obtain wealth showing us that He wants the people of the kingdom to be prosperous. With this in mind why would any follower of Christ think that God the Father has a problem with them having money or wealth? If God has a problem with money or wealth then that would be a contradiction of the above mentioned scripture and other verses in the bible that reference blessings from God. Keep in mind that God does not have a problem with money and wealth so let us look at the different success stories that are found in the bible.

Let us begin by looking at Adam and Eve the first man and woman who were on the earth living in the Garden of Eden. This man and his wife lived in a place that had an abundance of everything that they could ever want or need. It was a rich, beautiful place filled with nothing but the best from God. Ponder that for just a moment it had the best of everything it was not an average or mediocre place. Therefore, if God gave this first man and woman the best of and everything in great abundance then why would the heavenly Father want you and I to be broke, needy and in lack? That would go against what God shows us by creating a beautiful garden with everything in it. Christians need to change their mindset and attitude about money and wealth because God does not mind them having money and wealth. When we consider the scripture that leads into this chapter think about the fact that God owns everything and wants to put what He owns into the hands of His people. Understanding this should encourage believers to be excited about the opportunity be owners of houses, lands, businesses and much more. The devil has for far too long blinded God's people with the dumb idea that money and wealth are evil and frowned upon by God. It is time to have these blinders removed so that every follower of Christ can walk in wealth and fulfill the purpose of God for their lives. What has always amazed me about Christians and this debate on the issue of money and wealth is how many believers never look at the fact that Adam and Eve were living in a place filled with abundance. They seem to think that Adam and Eve were living in some average place which helps these believers to continue to insist that having money and wealth is a sin. No believer should want to commit sin but I feel it is a sin to not receive the promises of God and all their fullness for your life. Adam and Eve serve as the first example that God wants the best and abundance for those who are a member of the kingdom of God. You need to get this idea of God wanting you to have the best and let it sink deep into your mind. God wants to show the world through you how great a provider our heavenly Father can be to those who trust and believe in Him.

Next in our examples will be Abram who later had his name changed to Abraham who was a man of great faith that God directed to leave his family and journey to a new land. God the Father established a covenant with Abram and promised to not only bless this man but to multiply him as well. In reading about Abram's life in the book of Genesis you will find out that he was a very wealthy man who had great flocks, herds and servants. One verse of scripture states his wealth this way; *Genesis 13:2 (KJV) And Abram was very rich in cattle, in silver, and in gold.* Here is a man who has faith in God receiving riches and wealth and Abram had a nephew named Lot who was also traveling with him. Lot became rich and wealthy from being connected to his uncle and at one point because of the large herds and flocks that both men had. Their servants got into a heated argument over trying to care for the animals so Abram and Lot decided to separate because the land could not support both of their flocks and herds. When you have servants you need to have money or wealth to provide for them and for yourself which Abram was able to do. Abram received his riches and wealth because of his faith in God which proves that God is in the blessing business and does not have a problem with people having money or wealth. I do not understand how anyone could read about the life of Abram and then make the decision to believe that God hates money and wealth when it was the heavenly Father who provided the money and wealth in the first place. Every time I read about Abram and what God did for him I get excited and encouraged because the Father can and will do the same for me and for you if we just believe. His story is meant to encourage believers to want and expect great things from God because they believe and trust Him completely. Stop expecting or believing for little and ask for much because God can and will do it. Faith was the key for Abram and your faith is necessary for you to get money and wealth because God has them available for your life.

In going deeper into individuals who were wealthy next on my list would be Isaac who was the son that God promised Abram that would be his heir. Naturally after Abram dies Isaac inherits the majority of his father's remaining wealth although his half-brother Ishmael receives a portion as well. Isaac has wealth and continues to prosper while living in Gerar; *Genesis 26:12-14 (KJV) Then Isaac sowed in that land, and received in the same year a hundredfold: and the Lord blessed him. And the man waxed great, and went forward, and grew until he became very great: For he had possessions of flocks, and possession of herds, and great store of servants: and the Philistines envied him.* Again we can see from the scriptures that God the Father was the one responsible for Isaac's success. Therefore, we must acknowledge that God was the one blessing

Isaac further proving that our heavenly Father does not have a problem with godly people having money or wealth. Most people who are saved are like the Philistines and envious of rich and wealthy people when the unsaved people are supposed to be jealous of the prosperity of the believers. Many times Christians have overlooked and misunderstood money and wealth because they did not take the time to study the bible on this subject. God wants to put money and wealth into the hands of His people to do great things in the earth. Isaac had two sons Jacob and Esau who would receive portions of his wealth when he died and they both were prosperous and successful.

Another rich and wealthy man from the bible is Job who not only served God but was always faithful in his relationship to the heavenly Father. Most Christians know of the great suffering that Job endured but his wealth is often forgotten or overlooked. He was married with a large family of ten children seven sons and three daughters to be exact. With such a large family Job would definitely need a large amount of money or wealth to support and provide for his family and their needs. The bible tells us this about his money and wealth; *Job 1:3 (KJV) His substance also was seven thousand sheep, and three thousand camels, and five hundred yoke of oxen, and five hundred she asses, and a very great household; so that this man was the greatest of all the men of the east.* Job was the wealthiest man where he resided and by today's standards would have been considered a billionaire. Imagine that for just a moment here is Job a servant of God who is a billionaire which proves that God does not have a problem with money and wealth. Now I know that someone will read this statement and say well he also lost his children and his wealth while almost dying from an illness and that is true. However, the bible also shows us that after Job went through his personal tragedy that God gave this man even more than what was lost; *Job 42:12-13 (KJV) So the Lord blessed the latter end of Job more than his beginning: for he had fourteen thousand sheep, and six thousand camels, and a thousand yoke of oxen, and a thousand she asses. He had also seven sons and three daughters.* Anyone who believes that God has a problem with money and wealth should ask themselves if that is true then why did the heavenly Father give Job more than what was lost? God was the source of Job's money and wealth which I am sure was the result of this man having respect for the heavenly Father and refusing to do evil. Job lived his life the way he did which allowed God to pour out great blessings into his life. What we learn from the latter years of Job's life is that it is never too late and that we are never too old to receive money and wealth from God.

One of my favorite stories of someone going from rages to riches is found in the bible (2 Kings 4:1-7) which involves a woman who had recently become a widow and has two sons to take care of. However, because of her and her deceased husband's poor money management skills the creditors had arrived to take the sons as slaves to work and payoff the debt of their parents. If you have ever had creditors call you about overdue bills then you can relate to her situation. Then when all looks hopeless God shows up by sending Elisha a prophet who the woman tells about her situation seeking any help she can get. After hearing the woman's plight Elisha asks the widow what does she have in her house and she replies one pot of oil. Elisha then tells her to go and borrow as many pots as she can get from her neighbors, friends and family. Once she has borrowed as many pots as she can get then a miracle takes place as her and her sons pour oil from the original pot into all of the borrowed pots filling them. The woman is told by Elisha to take the oil and sell it to pay off her debt and to live off of the remaining money. Think about that for a moment and imagine her kitchen area filled with all sorts of pots in different shapes and sizes probably leaving little to no room to walk around in the kitchen. Not only is this a miracle but it also shows us how one word or idea from God can change someone's entire life for the better. God gave the woman the ability to get wealth which leads us to the conclusion that God does not want His people to be in lack and that He does not have a problem with them having money or wealth. I know that God will do the same for people today if they are willing to trust and believe in Him and be obedient. The widow received a word on what to do but she still had to make up her mind to be obedient and to follow the instructions of Elisha for the results to work in her favor. Ask yourself how many times has God given you an idea for something that would have changed your finances and you refused to be obedient and act on it. When you refuse to act or move by faith you miss out on an opportunity to have a miracle and great money or wealth being placed into your hands.

God is the one who provides money and wealth for His people and will open doors of opportunity such as what happened in the life David the young shepherd boy who would one day become a king. The nation of Israel was at war against their enemy the Philistines and both armies were in battle formation when a champion Philistine named Goliath put forth a personal challenge. This giant who was a great warrior called for an Israelite to challenge him so that they could fight one on one and the winner's nation would rule over the loser's. However, because of Goliath's great stature and reputation no one from Israel's army would accept the challenge. Saul who is the king decides to try and offer an incentive to encourage someone to step forward and makes an offer that whoever kills Goliath will receive a great amount of money. Along with that the man will also receive the king's daughter as a wife and their family will become exempt from taxes. David the shepherd boy is the youngest of his father's eight sons and has been sent by his dad to take some food to his three oldest brothers who are in the army and to return with a report about the battle. Arriving at the front line of the battle allows David to hear Goliath yelling threats against the army of God's people. Most people would say that David was there by coincidence but I believe that it was all part of God's bigger plan. I personally do not believe in coincidence because I know that God has a plan and often moves in ways that are not the ways or methods of man. David learns of the king's offer if someone kills Goliath but I believe that he was motivated not by the king's incentive but by anger over Goliath insulting the army and his nation. He is willing to take action and decides to take on Goliath in battle and eventually goes against the giant warrior with a slingshot. David coming to fight armed only with a slingshot causes Goliath to assume that he will quickly kill the young man however, things take a different course. Goliath is hit in the forehead with a stone from David's slingshot killing the Philistine instantly. Then the final insult is when David takes Goliath's own sword and cuts the Philistine's head off. God the Father gives us opportunities or situations where we can obtain money or wealth but there may be a giant or two that we have to slay in the process. Defeating Goliath brought David money, wealth, a wife, fame and exemption from taxes for his family. Everything that David was blessed to receive was designed by God for this young man's life and our heavenly Father wants to do the same for us today.

When I think of money and wealth Solomon who became the king of Israel after the death of his father David must be part of the discussion. Solomon was appointed king by his father shortly before David's death and was instructed by his father to keep the commands of God. In the beginning of his reign as king the bible tells us that Solomon loved the Lord with all his heart. One day Solomon went to Gibeon to offer sacrifices and during the night God appeared to him in a dream. In the dream Solomon was told by God that he could ask for anything that he desired. Just reading that let me know that God must have been really pleased with Solomon which is something that every believer should strive to do. I believe that most people if they were given the choice to ask for anything from God would have surely desired great amounts of money but, Solomon asked for wisdom. This request by Solomon was so pleasing to God because it showed that the king understood the value of or importance of wisdom. As a result of Solomon's request he also received what he did not ask for which is money. Confirmation that God does not have a problem with His people having money or wealth. It must be stated that all Christians need to ask God for wisdom in managing their money and wealth. We must understand that it is expected that a king will normally have money and wealth because they have citizens who will be paying taxes that go to support the nation or kingdom. In Solomon's situation having God make a promise to provide money and wealth in addition to what the king would normally receive means his wealth will exceed all the other kingdoms. The bible mentions that in one year Solomon received six hundred and sixty six talents of gold so we can see from this that great wealth was definitely in the hands of this king. Just imagine what you could do with that much gold if you had it. You could buy anything you wanted, build whatever you desire and travel anywhere you would like to go. There would be no limits in your life and how you live and that was certainly the case for Solomon because money was not an issue for him. Our heavenly Father desires for every believer to have no limits of what they can do in their lives.

Let us now look at the story of the Wise Men who learned of the birth of Jesus and traveled from a great distance just to worship Him. These men were carrying with them gold, myrrh and frankincense that they would give as an offering to the young child. Whatever wealth that Joseph and Mary already had would be greatly increased from the gifts that the Wise men were bringing. Myrrh and frankincense could be sold because it was used to make oils usually anointing oil and gold was a great for buying things. The idea of Joseph and Mary being poor and broke is destroyed once again by them receiving money and wealth. Joseph one night while sleeping is warned in a dream to take his family to Egypt because Herod wants kill his young son. The gold, myrrh and frankincense could provide the financial means to travel and money to live on while in a foreign country. Additional proof that God is the one who will provide money and wealth for His people. Let these examples from the bible encourage you to believe that God wants you to be greatly blessed with money and wealth.

Highlights/Notes

1. God wants His people to be prosperous.

2. God will open doors of opportunity for money and wealth.

3. God must be first in your life for money and wealth to occur.

4. There may be obstacles but God will help you to overcome them.

5. One idea from God can change your finances forever.

6. Obedience is necessary when God gives you an idea.

7. Ask God for wisdom to manage your money and wealth.

Chapter Four

God's Purpose for Money & Wealth

Bring ye all the tithes into the storehouse, that there may be meat in mine house, and prove me now herewith, saith the Lord of hosts, if I will not open you the windows of heaven, and pour you out a blessing, that there shall not be room enough to receive it.
Malachi 3:10 (KJV)

In this chapter we will discuss God's purposes for believers having money and wealth which are three reasons; first of all is for Christians to support financially their local church through the giving of tithes and offerings. Second, is for the believers to enjoy and to have a better quality of life for them and their families and third is to help others that are in need. I know that some of you are mad because I have mentioned the hated subject of giving money through tithes and offerings. People don't like being told what to do with their hard earned money and immediately think that the preacher is going to take all of their money and spend it on his or herself. Let me say this that just because a few preachers have misused church funds does not represent every pastor or minister. First and foremost the church needs money for it to operate daily paying its bills such as the rent, mortgage, utilities, salaries, accountants, lawyers, employees and to fulfill its divine assignment in various ministries like supplying food for the hungry and clothing for the naked. Job training for recently released prisoners or those looking for employment which takes money. I have had many discussions with Christians on the subject of tithing and giving offerings and it simply boils down to whether or not you want to obey God. Some believers have told me that because we are now under grace and not under the law that we are not required to tithe. On the other hand many people have told me that in tithing you are supposed to tithe from the net amount of your paycheck and not the gross but I remind them that Abram gave a tithe of all that he recovered after rescuing Lot and the others that were taken captive. When I first became a believer I had to deal with this issue of tithing and giving offerings for myself because I thought ten percent was a lot of money and wondered how I would pay my bills. At the beginning of my Christian journey I started with half of what I was supposed to give because I was new to tithing and afraid but within a year's time I began to give ten percent of my gross earnings. I had to grow as a new believer and build my faith and understand that God would honor me for tithing. Tithes and offerings are what churches need to help them in doing the work of ministry for God. The above mentioned scripture shows that God promises to do His part when we do our part in supporting and taking care of the local church. As a member of a local church it is you're responsibility to not just to come to church and bible study but to give your money in support of that organization. There is a great example of the people of Israel supporting the ministry which occurred when Moses asked them to freely give the materials necessary in making the items for the tabernacle (Exodus 36). The people were so faithful in their giving that an offering was brought daily by the people. Their giving was so great to the ministry that there was an excess of items and Moses had to ask them to stop giving. Here is a wonderful example of God's people understanding that their money and wealth were needed to be used to support the ministry. I have been a Christian for many years and as a pastor I have conducted and been a part of many worship services. However, I have never been involved in one where the people gave so much that they were asked to stop giving. Imagine for just a moment if the believers supported the local church as they should then those churches would have greater financial resources to accomplish more for God's kingdom. Those same churches would not have to always seek financial assistance from banks or it would reduce the amount of the loans needed from those lending institutions.

Let us also look at Jesus giving the Temple tax which was required of all Jewish males twenty years or older which was to be done on a yearly basis. The fact that our Lord Jesus gave serves as additional proof that Christians are supposed to give their tithes and offerings to support the work of their local church. If you do not give your tithes and offerings to your local church why would you expect God to give to you when you are showing Him that you do not care about what He cares about. From the book of Malachi and the scripture that I started this chapter with the prophet Malachi was addressing the people of Israel about not taking care of God's house. Solomon used a portion of his vast money and wealth to not only build his own house but to build the Temple of God for worship and the wall of Jerusalem. He was concerned about the things of God just as much as he was concerned about his own personal things. Make sure that you are taking care of your local church and watch how God will take care of you. I must give you one more important point which is your attitude in the giving of your tithes and offerings which should be done with joy and not by complaining. The bible tells us how important our attitude is in giving and that by being joyful not only pleases God but allows us to receive blessings in return which is why Paul writes about being a cheerful giver in his epistle to the Corinthian churches. Most of the time when an offering is asked for in a church service many people give but with the wrong attitude. Cheerful giving pleases God who is our source. As believers we must be excited and happy to give financially to our local church because this allows our heavenly Father to release money, wealth and other things into our lives.

The second purpose for money and wealth is for you to use it to enjoy a better quality and standard of living for you and your family. Once again I must mention tithing for a moment because it allows God to take care of or provide for your needs. There is a story in the bible found in 1 Kings 17:8-16 that illustrates this point. Elijah who is a prophet has been instructed by God to go to Zarephath because a woman who is a widow will provide for the prophet. After Elijah arrives in Zarephath he spots the widow outside the gates of the city gathering sticks. During a brief conversation with the widow Elijah asks her to bring him some water and a morsel of bread. She responds to his request by informing Elijah that all she has at home is a handful of meal and a little oil in a jar and that she plans to prepare one last meal for herself and her son. Hearing her situation and plans causes Elijah to tell the widow that if she will feed him first by giving him a small cake that God promises to make sure that her food supply will not run out. Elijah was asking her to give a tithe of all she had because the tithe is a tenth or small portion and for the widow to believe that God would supply her needs by her giving first. Fortunately the widow believes and receives the word spoken by God through Elijah just as a Christian agrees to give a tenth to God first. Her faith is in God and the word that she has received and by giving the tithe in the form of a small cake the widow's food supply never stops flowing. God always wants to provide or take care of the needs of His people.

God wants you to have nice things and to enjoy life to the full and the bible speaks on this; *3 John 2 (KJV) Beloved, I wish above all things that thou mayest prosper and be in health, even as thy soul prospereth.* It is a part of God's plan for the believer to grow financially as they grow spiritually. What a wonderful thing it is that God wants us to grow or to increase in every way possible. Our heavenly Father wants us to have nice houses, cars, clothes, and to take our families out to fancy restaurants and to go on great vacations. I know that some of you who read this will disagree because you have a difficult time believing that God wants you to enjoy your life. You have been taught for so long that money and wealth are evil that you cannot see yourself having fun in your life. If you will listen I can tell you that you need to embrace these words of a better life so that you can make the most of and enjoy your life. Right now today this very moment it is time for you to start living and to stop watching others enjoy life. When you are not enjoying and making the most out of your life then you become angry when you see others having fun. Some Christians have taken vows of poverty which does not make them holier than others and it does not bring them closer to God. Jesus paid a heavy price not just on the cross for our salvation but for each of us to have a more abundant and prosperous life. Abraham enjoyed a life of prosperity and that same life is available to each of us today. You must believe by faith that you are a joint heir in the kingdom of God and that the promises of blessings of money and wealth belong to you.

The third reason for you to have money and wealth is to leave and inheritance to future generations along with helping others that are in need. We must strive to be blessed and in return be a blessing to others helping to improve their lives. When Abram or Abraham died he left his wealth to his sons Isaac and Ishmael and their children which if used wisely would make life better for those generations of descendants. Christians should be concerned about leaving money and wealth for future generations to help them have a better quality of life. We see this biblical principle practiced by wealthy people in the world who have left their money and wealth to help their families for the future. It is my desire to leave not just a positive legacy but money and wealth for the generations that come after me. Scripture speaks clearly about leaving an inheritance to future generations; *Proverbs 13:22 (KJV) A good man leaveth an inheritance to his children's children: and the wealth of the sinner is laid up for the just.* This verse of scripture contains two important things that believers need to understand about money and wealth. Which are that they should strive to help future generations in their families by sowing good financial seeds in the present and that sinners or the unsaved have money and wealth that God wants to put back into the hands of His people. I cannot stress this point enough that God does not have a problem with money and wealth and desires to place it in the hands of Christians who will use it wisely. There is a parable in the bible that Jesus uses to illustrate the point about helping others with your money and wealth titled The Good Samaritan (Luke 10:25-37). In this parable there was a man who was traveling from

Jerusalem to Jericho who was robbed and beaten severely by thieves who left the man near death. Along comes a priest who sees the man and does not offer any help but walks on the other side of the road to avoid the injured man. Next comes along a Levite who does the same thing that the priest did and passes the injured by walking on the other side of the road. After the priest and Levite have passed then along comes a Samaritan who not only stops to help the injured man but takes that man to an inn where he can safely recover from his injures. The Samaritan did more than just help to rescue the injured man because he also paid for the injured man's lodging or medical expenses. You must understand that Jews and Samaritans where not friends but enemies so having the Samaritan help the injured man when a priest and Levite should have was an insult. We can see that the Samaritan fulfilled the command of God by caring for his neighbor and it should have angered the Jewish people for neglecting one of their own. I wonder how many times the followers of Christ have acted like the priest and Levite by not offering help when they have had the opportunity to do so.

Sometimes people who are in a position to help others either miss an opportunity or refuse to provide assistance for another person that is in need as was the case with the Rich Man and Lazarus as told by Jesus in the sixteenth chapter of the Gospel of Luke. In that story the Rich Man had the means to not only feed Lazarus who was hungry but the ability to provide for this man to get treatment for the sores on his body. The Rich Man chose to ignore Lazarus and his suffering and we see this same mentally or meanness in people today who turn a blind eye to others that are on hard times. When the love of God is inside of you then you are bothered by seeing the suffering of others and will try to use your money and wealth to help them while they are going through a low point in life. Anyone can fall on hard times and we must remember that because we could be in their shoes hoping that someone will give us a hand up.

Christians are supposed to be people who not only talk about helping their neighbor but follow through with action. There are several examples of the believers in the early Christian church using their money and wealth to help other believers who were in lack. We find one such occasion mentioned in scripture, *Acts 2:44-45 (KJV) And all that believed were together, and had all things common; And sold their possessions and goods, and parted them to all men, as every man had need.* The behavior of these early believers was much different than that of the rich young man who was told by Jesus to sell all his possessions and to give the money to the poor. It is important to make a side by side comparison of his actions verses the individuals of the early church. These new Christians were more than willing to part with their possessions to help others when the rich young man would never consider such a thing. I wonder how many Christians today that would be willing to sell some of what they have to help ours that are in lack. As a Christian it is part of our responsibility and duty that we care about the needs and well-being of others not just those who share our faith in Christ but all people. The early church believers were selfless and the act of selling their possessions and sharing the proceeds with others is proof. We can see through their actions that the love of God was truly inside of them and that they were going to be a blessing to others. Truly this was an act of God's love on the part of those individuals who were willing to make life better for others who were less fortunate. On one of his missionary journeys Paul had asked for the believers of the churches in Galatia and Corinth to take up a collection for the struggling believers in the Jerusalem church. Churches today should help one another because we serve the same God and are on the same team. Every church today needs to follow the examples of the early believers in the book of Acts and model their caring spirit after the churches in Galatia and Corinth. Even John the beloved disciples addresses the issue of believers giving to help others; *1 John 3:17 (KJV) But whoso hath this world's good, and seeth his brother have need, and shutteth up his bowels of compassion from him, how dwelleth the love of God in him?.* John is confirming that God wants His children to use their money and wealth to help others and by believers doing this shows that the love of God resides in them. People will often say that they love someone but love is not just with words that are spoken but by the actions of the one making the statement.

A final story of someone being selfish and not using their money or wealth to help others would come from the Parable of the Rich Fool (Luke 12:16-21). In this particular parable Jesus talks about a Rich Man who has a bountiful harvest of crops who needs more storage space. The Rich Man decides that in order to solve his problem that he will tear down his existing barns and build new larger ones. Once this has been done the Rich Man decides that he will just sit back, relax and enjoy what he has achieved without a concern for others around him that may be less fortunate. Jesus then says that the heavenly Father speaks to the Rich Man telling him that he will die and then his grain or wealth will belong to others. What needs to emphasized is that the Rich Man was not interested in using his money and wealth to help the work of God's kingdom, or to help others that were in need. He just wanted to keep all of his money and wealth for himself. In other words the Rich Man of the parable was extremely selfish or self-centered. God the Father does not want his people to be selfish or self-centered but to be the kind of individuals who have a heart for Him and other human beings. Make sure that as God blesses you with money and wealth that you do not forget about your responsibility to help the work of God's kingdom or other people. Tomorrow is not promised to any of us and we can be here today and gone the next day and our money and wealth will fall into someone else's hands. And that person may use it wisely doing God's will or foolishly solely for their own gain.

Many people today use a portion of their money and wealth to help those that are less fortunate by giving to non-profit organizations that meet the needs of the homelessness, people who suffer from drugs and that have been abused and so forth. I have been giving a portion of my money for several years to a non-profit organization because I like and agree with the services that they provide to families who have children that are battling cancer. By giving a portion of my money or wealth to this organization I am sharing what God has blessed me to have to provide for someone else's needs. And I am not alone in giving to these non-profits organizations because there are multitudes of people who give yearly to these great organizations. Now I must give a word of caution because you must do some research on any organization that you plan on giving money. Ensuring that most if not all of your money is actually used for the organization's cause and not just going to assist with administrative costs. You giving your money and wealth to help the less fortunate will not only improve the lives of others but it will please our heavenly Father.

Highlights/Notes

1. Use your money and wealth to support the local church.

2. Use your money and wealth to enjoy your life.

3. Plan to leave a portion of your money and wealth to future generations.

4. Use your money and wealth to help the less fortunate.

5. God wants you to prosper in every area of your life.

6. Set a standard of giving and encourage others to follow.

7. God blesses His children to be a blessing to others.

Chapter Five

Make Money Work for You

And unto one he gave five talents, to another two, and to another one; to every man according to his several ability; and straightway took his journey.
Matthew 25:15 (KJV)

It is important for Christians to understand that God wants His people to use their money and wealth so that it will continue to generate a return as they invest it wisely. You should be looking at stocks, bonds, mutual funds, real estate properties, business ventures and other potential opportunities to put your money and wealth to work for you. There will always be a level of risk involved when you invest your money and wealth so you must be aware of that and consider it as you look for potential opportunities. We have all heard the failure stories of someone who invested their money or wealth in a promising stock or upstart business only to lose most if not all of what they invested. Similarly we have also heard the success stories of someone who invested their money and wealth and made a fortune. Investing your money and wealth could mean starting your own business or partnering with an existing business as a method to grow your money and wealth. Whatever you decide to invest in it is important that you consider the risks and the rewards.

In the bible there is a story that Jesus uses to teach about investing money found in Matthew's gospel called The Parable of the Talents. This story begins with a wealthy man who has decided to go away on a trip but before he departs the wealthy man gives his three servants different amounts of money based on their ability. Think of the wealthy man as someone giving a stockbroker their money to invest with hopes of receiving a huge return. The wealthy man is taking a big risk by giving his servants money hoping that he will have a sizable return on his initial investment. He starts by giving the first servant five talents, the second servant is given two talents while the last servant is given one talent. Then we are told that the servant with five talents went and was able to trade and increase his amount by gaining five more talents. And that the servant who was given two talents was able to increase his by gaining an additional two talents. However, the servant who received one talent did nothing and simply took his master's money and hid it in the ground. When the wealthy man returns from his trip he checks with his servants to see what they have done with the money that they were each given. As the servants are making their reports to the wealthy man, he is pleased to learn that the first two servants have doubled his money while third servant did nothing and returned the original amount of money that he was given. Hearing that the third servant did nothing with the money angered the wealthy man who gave the servant a severe rebuke. A rebuke was necessary because the money could have been put in the bank where it would have gained some interest for the wealthy man. Sadly most Christians are like the third servant and do nothing with their money or wealth.

The bible has examples of people putting their money or wealth to work for them by purchasing real estate. One of the first examples that I would like to discuss comes from the life of Abraham. Sarah the wife of Abraham has died and this man not only has to deal with the pain of her passing but plan the funeral. He needs a place to bury his beloved wife and decides to purchase some land so a meeting is arranged between Abraham and Ephron. Where an agreement can be made so that Abraham can purchase the necessary land for a burial plot. This is what people do today when someone dies they meet with a funeral director who makes arrangements for a burial plot to be purchased for the deceased to be laid to rest in. Abraham and Ephron agree on a price of four hundred shekels of silver and in exchange Abraham would receive a field that had many trees and a cave that would serve as a family burial plot. Now with the purchase completed and the transaction recorded. One way that Abraham could receive a return on his investment would be by leasing the field and possibly cutting some of the trees and selling it as lumber. I believe that this story shows us that investing in land or real estate is a good way to make our money and wealth work for us.

Next would be a story that comes from the life of Jeremiah who is often referred to as the weeping prophet. This mighty prophet receives instructions from God at a time when the Babylonian army has surrounded Jerusalem and he is being held prisoner in the king of Judah's house. Jeremiah's nephew comes to the prison requesting that Jeremiah redeem or purchase the land that he has. God the Father confirms that Jeremiah should purchase the field of Anathoth and the price that is agreed upon is seventeen shekels of silver and the transaction is recorded. What is interesting in this purchase is that many of the people of Jerusalem are about to go into captivity once the Babylonian army seizes the entire city. However, when the people eventually return to the land Jeremiah will still be the owner of this property which was to confirm one of his prophecies that the people would one day return to their homeland. The prophet having the deed to the land would give Jeremiah many opportunities to make a return on his investment by renting, leasing or selling it in the future. Real estate is a way to make your money or wealth work for you and if you doubt that then just look at the many shows on television where people are buying houses and flipping them for a profit. Several years ago I attended some workshops on purchasing real estate with my wife as we looked at ways to increase our income. My wife always wanted to have different real estate properties as a way of making our money and wealth to work for us. We looked at rental properties and consulted with a lawyer on the good and bad of having tenants. You must do more than just talk about investing your money and wealth by actively seeking to gain knowledge before you sign any contracts or documents.

Putting your money in the bank will allow it to accumulate some interest which is a way to let your money work for you. Many believers spend what money or wealth that they do have on items that do not accumulate in value or add financial increase. Buying the latest cellphone, car, or designer clothes may seem like a great idea but they do not increase your money or wealth. Those items will quickly depreciate in value as other items hit the market. Wealthy people look for opportunities to grow their money and wealth and this same biblical principal needs to be applied by God's people. Our heavenly Father wants believers to grow not just spiritually in knowledge of Him but financially with their money and wealth. I believe it is time for every believer to fully understand this and to be diligent in looking for ways to increase their money and wealth through investing. We must do some homework to find opportunities that will put us on the path to greater financial success. I want to note or mention here that God's children need to teach their children about managing money and wealth along with investing it. The only way to break the curse of lack and poverty for future generations is by believers starting early as possible in teaching their children about money and wealth. Financial information that is shared early on may be the difference for our future descendants having a better life so we must do all that we can now to assist them. Let me go back to someone who was mentioned in a previous chapter the Rich Young Ruler (Mark 10:17-31). We are not given much information about this young man, nothing on his family background, exact age or how he became rich. However, we do know that he had become successful and accumulated a substantial amount of money and wealth. He could have been between twenty one and twenty five years of age which is what most people today would consider as a young successful entrepreneur. What I also think is important to note is that this rich young ruler had a powerful determination and drive to achieve success. It is my belief that in order for him to achieve it all started at home and that one or both of his parents took the time to teach him about money and wealth. This reminds me of the scripture; *Proverbs 22:6 (KJV) Train up a child in the way he should go: and when he is old, he will not depart from it.* Teaching our children about God and His ways along with scriptures on money and wealth is extremely important. Train our children about money and wealth early so that their lives can be prosperous. Unfortunately most of our children or young people do not learn about money and wealth at home and it is not taught in schools. Then many of these young people go to college where card credits are offered and they apply receiving them and end up with tremendous amounts of debt. Make sure that in this modern era of phone apps to transfer money and to pay bills online that your children know how to fill out a check properly, balance a checkbook and that they can read a bank statement. There are children who do not know how to fill out a check or to balance a checkbook which means that they will be in trouble for their lack of knowledge. As a parent you need to make certain that you have done all that you can to arm your children with knowledge about money wealth. If we do not teach our children how to manage their money and wealth then they will not have any for the future. The bible makes mention of this; *Proverbs 21:20 (KJV) There is treasure to be desired and oil in the dwelling of the wise; but a foolish man spendeth it up.* When our children lack wisdom and knowledge about money and wealth they will always spend it and never save for a rainy day. No parent wants their child to learn the lessons of life the hard way. Spend some quality time teaching your children and grandchildren about the value of and importance of money and wealth. Life can be difficult but not having knowledge about money and wealth can make it even more trying or stressful. Not training our children about money and wealth can have a negative impact on their lives for many years. I believe that Abram prepared his son Isaac for financial success at a young and continued to teach those lessons into adulthood. Financial success in the areas of money and wealth are included in the promises of God to His people. Serving God with our whole hearts through faith creates an atmosphere where the promises for a brighter financial future are available and will manifest in our lives. Lastly I would like to encourage every believer to pray seeking guidance from God before investing your money and wealth. Our heavenly Father will confirm whether the opportunities we are considering are sound choices toward the financial success that we desire to have. It is important to always seek guidance from God the Father because He knows all things. We should never want to make major decisions in our lives without first consulting God. He has promised to always direct our path but we must seek Him first. Investing money will always have a level of risk associated with it but I trust God the Father will steer me clear of any pitfalls and obstacles. I look forward to greater financial growth in my life so that I can help the kingdom of God.

Highlight/Notes

1. God wants His people to put their money to work for them.

2. Look for sound investments for your money to work for you.

3. You must do your homework before investing your money.

4. You must chose to invest over spending your money.

5. Wealthy people look for opportunities to grow their money and wealth.

6. Poor people spend their money on depreciable goods.

7. Financial increase must become not only a mindset but a way of life.

Chapter Six

God is a God of Increase

And the Lord make you to increase and abound in love one toward another, and toward all men, even as we do toward you.
1 Thessalonians 3:12 (KJV)

Hopefully by now you are starting to understand that through your faith, God really does want to bring increase into every area of your life. Our heavenly Father wants His people to increase spiritually as well as financially which is what Paul was addressing in the above scripture. God likes to increase His children so we must believe that and be willing to do what is necessary to receive all of our wonderful blessings. In the previous chapters of this book I gave many examples of people who received financial increase from God. Their faith allowed these men and women to receive money and wealth which should serve as evidence for believers today. It is the believers who should realize that God loves to bless or increase His people. However, many Christians are still hung up on the idea of money and wealth being bad or evil. The idea of God being a God of increase should not surprise believers because He does this from a heart of love. We must remember that God the Father gave us the greatest gift ever His Son Jesus and when we truly understand the value of this gift then why would our Father withhold financial increase from us?

A great example of God promising to give increase can be found in the book of Joshua. For those of you who are not familiar with Joshua's story he was selected by God to lead the Israelites into the Promised Land after Moses' death. We find God once again proving that He wants to give His people increase by the following scripture. *Joshua 1:8 (KJV) This book of the law shall not depart out of thy mouth; but thou shalt meditate therein day and night, that thou mayest observe to do according to all that is written therein: for then thou shalt make thy way prosperous, and then thou shalt have good success.* Joshua is told that as long as he follows God's instructions then he will have success or increase in his life. The heavenly Father was taking the Israelites from slavery and a period of wilderness wandering into a land flowing with milk and honey that certainly sounds like increase to me. Most Christians read the bible and think that it talks only about faith but this view causes many believers to miss the other gems in the word of God. Those same instructions given to Joshua apply to all believers today who are willing to receive it by faith then they too can have good success or increase. If you are still not convinced that God is a God of increase then think about Joshua leading the people as they prepare to take the city of Jericho. Joshua and the people are instructed to march around the city and when the trumpet sounds the walls of the city to fall to the ground. Allowing the Israelites to plunder the city which they did taking silver, gold, and vessels of brass and iron that were put into the Lord's treasury. There is no other way to explain this other than God gave increase to His people. In the bible there is a scripture that helps us to understand one of God's ways for increase; *Proverbs 13:22a (KJV) the wealth of the sinner is laid up for the just.* The wealth of the sinners of Jericho was placed into the hands of the people of Israel. God has unlimited ways to bring financial increase into the lives of those who trust and believe in Him.

Another example of God giving increase comes from the life of Solomon when the heavenly Father told this man to ask for whatever he wanted to receive. Solomon loved God and when given the opportunity to receive whatever he wanted he did not ask for long life, fame, money or the death of his enemies but requested wisdom. Now we must be honest most people including myself would more than likely have asked for money. However, Solomon did not rush to make a decision and thought about what he really wanted and needed. This request for wisdom greatly pleased God who responded to Solomon this way; *1 Kings 3:13 (KJV) And I have also given thee that which thou hast not asked, both riches, and honor: so that there shall not be any among the kings like unto thee all thy days.* Increase is given to Solomon further showing us that God wants to bless His people. Furthermore, there is a conservation that God has with Abraham that also proves that the heavenly Father wants to bring increase into the lives of His people. *Genesis 22:17 (KJV) That in blessing I will bless thee, and in multiplying I will multiply thy seed as the stars of the heaven, and as the sand which is upon the seashore; and thy seed shall possess the gate of his enemies;.* Imagine the jubilation that Abraham must have felt at hearing these words from the heavenly Father. God the Father spoke this directly to Abraham and the word multiply means increase for Abraham and his descendants. I hope that you are getting the picture that as a Christian that you should expect to receive increase in your life from God. Think about this scripture for a moment; *Psalm 23:5 (KJV) Thou preparest a table before me in the presence of mine enemies: thou anointest my head with oil; my cup runneth over.* God wants your enemies or haters to see the increase that He gives you so that you will praise Him for it. Also this verse tells us that our cup will overflow which is once again proof that increase is available to you and me. One final example from the life of a man named Jabez who prayed asking God the Father to increase his territory. Jabez approached the heavenly Father in prayer asking for increase and guess what he received it which brings to mind the following scripture. Jesus spoke these words, *Matthew 7:7 (KJV) Ask, and it shall be given you; seek, and ye shall find; knock, and it shall be opened unto you.* We must be bold like Jabez who asked, sought, found, knocked and received from God the Father the increase of his territory. There is another scripture that God speaks through the prophet Jeremiah that mentions increase for the nation of Israel. That particular scripture is; *Jeremiah 29:11 (KJV) For I know the thoughts that I think toward you, saith the*

Lord, thoughts of peace, and not of evil, to give you an expected end. God was informing the people that His plan was to bless and prosper them and those same words apply to the followers of Christ today. By now you should be excited about the fact that God is a God of increase and realize that it is time for you to be on the receiving end of this increase. The heavenly Father has been waiting for you to believe so that He can release increase into your hands and life. I hope that you are now convinced that increase is ready and available for you to use and enjoy. Grab hold of this new revelation and take it because now is your time to act and there is no limit or boundaries to what you will be capable of achieving. A new era in your life is about to break forth and things are turning in your favor.

Highlights/Notes

1. Christians are supposed to experience increase in every area of their lives.

2. Joshua was told if he followed God's instructions he would receive increase.

3. God gave increase when the Israelites plundered the city of Jericho.

4. The Israelites going from slavery to the Promised Land was increase.

5. God wants our enemies to see the increase that we receive in our lives.

6. Every believer should expect to receive increase when they trust God.

7. God has unlimited ways to give His people increase and success.

Chapter Seven

As You Think

For as a he thinketh in his heart, so is he: Eat and drink, saith he to thee; but his heart not with thee.
Proverbs 23:7 (KJV)

It is important for you to understand that how you think about a subject plays a major role in whether or not you will receive positive results and that applies to the idea of receiving money and wealth in your life. As I previously stated if you believe that money and wealth are evil or bad then you will never receive the increase that God the Father has for you. If you see yourself as someone who will always be poor, broke and miserable then you will never receive increase. When you doubt or do not believe the promises of God then you will never receive what has been promised to you. We must transform our thoughts to that of fully believing that the promises of God are for us as blood washed born again followers of Christ. You cannot afford to let doubt creep into your thoughts because it will keep you stuck, depressed and always broke. Do not focus on your circumstances of a difficult childhood or of not having the same opportunities as others because God the Father is a miracle worker who can do the impossible.

One of the stories I want to look at for a moment comes from the life of Moses when the heavenly Father was calling this man for leadership.

Moses had a stuttering problem and when God the Father tells him to go and address the elders of Israel. He replies to God asking how can he address the elders when he has trouble speaking clearly. The problem was that Moses saw himself as just someone who stutters and forgot that God the Father could fix that problem for him. Many believers are like Moses they only see their problem but they forget that our heavenly Father is the problem solver. God the Father corrects Moses' speech problem and now he can go and address not only the elders of Israel but Pharaoh the king. In a way Moses having his stuttering problem fixed could be seen as him receiving increase in his life. If Moses did not receive healing for his speech problem he never would have become the mighty leader that he developed into. His confidence in God the Father and in himself changed when the speech problem was corrected.

Next I wanted to go back to Jabez because here was a man whose named meant pain however, he refused to let the meaning of his name deter him from a better and brighter future. Jabez did not see himself as someone who should suffer with or cause pain all of his life. He dared to believe and saw himself differently when most people in his situation would have just accepted that they were supposed to have a troubled life. He shows us that our lives do not have to be filled with or cause pain to others. This man saw himself, his life and his future as being positive rather than negative. How do you see yourself and your life? If you see yourself and your life as negative then you will never receive anything good and especially not money and wealth. You must see yourself like Jabez saw himself and say that you will not be miserable but live a good life with more than enough money and wealth. A positive attitude even at the worst of times in life will keep you encouraged to believe that things will change in your favor.

Another story that I want to mention comes from a man named Gideon who lived during a time when his homeland suffered oppression by the Midianites. An angel of God told Gideon that he was a mighty man of valor and that God was with him however, Gideon only saw the suffering of his people. He felt like the stories of old about God the Father rescuing and providing for the people were not true so Gideon did not believe he would become a mighty man of valor. Not only was Gideon focused on the suffering of the people but he was from a poor family and knew nothing only hard times. Gideon was focused on everything negative which is what people tend to do in life always talking negatively and not expecting things to change. The bible even tells us this; *Proverbs 18:21 (KJV) Death and life are in the power of the tongue: and they that love it shall eat the fruit thereof.* We must be careful at all times and watch what we say because our words can produce life or death for us. This future military leader did not believe that he could do anything because of his circumstances. God then speaks to Gideon about him leading the army and defeating the Midianites. It took a lot of convincing before Gideon would believe God's plan for his life because he asked for several signs to confirm the heavenly Father's words. Upon receiving confirmation Gideon does finally agree to lead the army in battle and reduces his initial forces down to just three hundred troops. Gideon and his forces are greatly outnumbered but God the Father is with him and he defeats the Midianite forces soundly. Christians must learn to see themselves as our heavenly Father sees us as mighty men and women who can accomplish great things. Many Christians have often seen themselves in a negative way and that has to change before God can use us for His glory. You must see yourself as a wealthy man or woman of God before you receive money and wealth into your life. Believe that it is fine with God the Father for you to have money and wealth and that you will do good things with what is placed in your hands. You are created in the spiritual image of God so no longer view yourself as less than because you are valuable. Your life has been transformed so it does not matter where you started but where and how you finish is what counts. Whatever you lack God can supply so embrace a new day with excitement your future will be prosperous.

Highlights/Notes

1. Visualize yourself having money and wealth.

2. You must not allow doubt to creep into your thoughts.

3. You must not allow your past circumstances to cause unbelief.

4. You must see yourself and your life in a positive light.

5. You must not spend time focusing on your faults.

6. God the Father sees you as winner and you must see yourself this way.

7. You must keep a positive attitude no matter the circumstance.

Chapter Eight

Prosperity Preaching

Give, and it shall be given unto you; good measure, pressed down, and shaken together, and running over, shall men give into your bosom. For with the same measure that ye mete withal it shall be measured to you again.
Luke 6:38 (KJV)

I must spend time on the controversial subject of prosperity preaching because this thought or idea is the reason why many Christians fight against believing that God wants them to have money or wealth. Prosperity preaching started to come about in the 1950's when some preachers began to speak that Christians should believe that financial blessings and physical well-being are all a part of God's plan for the lives of His people. Those who preach and believe in the prosperity message also feel that it is important to give financially to their local church and other religious causes. Furthermore, the prosperity message views the bible as a contract between God and mankind. This doctrine stresses that personal empowerment is God's will for His people to be blessed in their lives. Now that we have an understanding of what the prosperity message is all about let us look at whether or not this is scriptural. Based on the information that I have previously provided throughout the pages of this book prosperity preaching is God's will for His people. You have spent a great deal of time reading this book and have looked at the many examples that I have used in this book that came directly from the bible. Hopefully you are convinced that God wants you to have an abundant life. God desires for you to have faith in Him, have a healthy physical body, have a sound mind, and have healthy relationships with people and to have money and wealth. Jesus did not die on the cross for His followers to spend their entire lives being poor, broke, depressed and miserable. The bible is a book of prosperity that covers every area of a person's life if they are willing to believe it and apply its words to their lives. I am often saddened when I hear Christians speak against having money and wealth because they believe that God hates rich and successful people. Nothing could be further from the truth the heavenly Father loves to see His people living well and doing great things. He takes pride in the success of His people when they give Him credit for providing them with money, wealth and success. However, many of God's people continue to struggle with and fight against the prosperity message spending their lives in lack financially and in other areas as well. What a shame it is for someone to accept Jesus as their personal Lord and Savior only to reject a portion of the promises in the bible. No one who has faith should want to live and not experience all of the rich blesses financially and otherwise that God has for them. I believe that God is moving like never before and opening doors to money and wealth for His people so that in these last days and times more people can be reached with gospel of Christ. Those that are in lack will experience God's love as He provides for their needs by using Christians who will set the example of giving for the world to follow. As the people of God give to and provide for the needs of others the heavenly Father will bless them with money and wealth to live an enjoyable life right now. God loves to give and when Christians give it touches His heart and causes the heavenly Father to give to them. Our heavenly Father is the ultimate giver because when He gave Jesus for the sins of mankind. It showed without a doubt that God will give to His people all that they need which includes money and wealth.

One of the issues with the prosperity message and those who preach about it are the material items and wealth that some have gained. Many people within the Christian community and outside of it feel that these preachers have taken the money of the poor members of the congregation and used it for their own personal benefit. What I feel is a part of this issue is jealousy because most people whether saved or not are angry when someone achieves a level of success. This same jealousy is seen when a professional athlete uses their platform in sports to speak out about a particular issue. The people who are against this athlete speaking out will often call them ungrateful and it is really that they are jealous of the athlete making millions of dollars. Now there have been some preachers who have taken advantage of church members financially but there are corporate executives who have done the same in the business world. There are many men and women who are preachers that work hard in ministry and in the secular world. Some even have their own businesses which helps them to achieve their goals of receiving money and wealth. I expect people who are not saved to be against Christians having money and wealth but when believers are against biblical prosperity it is shocking. One idea from God can change a Christian's financial future if they act on it and follow through with the instructions from God. Personally I know many believers who are ministers and entrepreneurs that are experiencing prosperity in money and wealth. Should these individuals pass up an opportunity to achieve their dreams of financial freedom because others will say that they are stealing from their members? The answer of course is no because they deserve the chance to pursue business opportunities outside of the church. As long as these preachers are not exploiting their church financially they deserve to be paid for their hard work and to use the money they earn however they see fit. When a person works and receives their paycheck they have the right to spend the money on whatever they want. We must not assume that when a preacher buys a new car that the money was misused funds from the church and that maybe they saved their money for a period of time before making the purchase. Confusion about the prosperity message has caused many believers to think that every luxury item that a preacher has obtained was done so with the use of illegal church funds. God the Father wants to prosper His people but in the proper way. Prosperity preaching is biblical and should not be a debatable issue but I know that this back and forth on the subject will continue until Jesus returns. Each Christian has to make up his or her own mind as to whether or not prosperity is from God and a part of His plan for their lives. As for me I believe it is a part of the plan for my life. I receive it and embrace it by faith and will not let someone convince me otherwise. There were many years of my Christian walk that I believed it was wrong for a believer to have great amounts of money and wealth. Lack of information and understanding kept me in the strangle hold of debt and depression but knowledge and truth has unlocked the door to a great future that I am supposed to have. The prophet Hosea even spoke about the people of God perishing for a lack of knowledge and that is what I experienced for many years concerning money and wealth. Perishing because I did not know that God wanted me to prosper financially because I believed that the heavenly Father hated money and wealth. How many other believers are missing out on the life that they are supposed to be living? I believe that there are others who are struggling and praying for a better understanding of prosperity looking for a change in their finances. God the Father has been prospering His people since the beginning of time. With this in mind know that He is willing to provide for your prosperity as long as you follow His plan and always acknowledge Him for every blessing. Please let God help you to change your mind about prosperity so that you do not spend years depressed and in debt. The devil will always send someone who will do their best to try and convince you that it is wrong or evil for you to have money and wealth. Walk away from them as quickly as you can before the negativity of their words causes doubt to seep into mind.

Highlights/Notes

1. The prosperity message is a controversial subject within the church community.

2. Financial blessings and physical health are a part of God's plan.

3. Prosperity should be experienced in every area of a Christian's life.

4. Misinformation causes many Christians to doubt the prosperity message.

5. The prosperity message is biblical and scriptural based.

6. Christians can perish financially for a lack of knowledge.

7. Study the scriptures to learn about biblical prosperity.

Chapter Nine

Loans & Credit Cards

The rich ruleth over the poor, and the borrower is servant to the lender.
Proverbs 22:7 (KJV)

As I begin this chapter I must make it clear that I am not in any way or form offering financial advice but giving you food for thought in managing your money and wealth. In the above scripture it tells us plainly that when we are the borrower that we become a servant to the one who loaned us money. However, the word servant is better translated slave because that is its Hebrew meaning and throughout history slaves have never been treated with kindness. It is important to talk about loans and credit cards because millions of people in this country are struggling financially from being over extended with loans and credit card debt. Loans are deeply woven into the fabric of our society because most people have or have had one of the major three loans which are student loans, car loans or a mortgage. I do understand why most people get loans because they may work a great distance from home and need a reliable form of transportation to go to and from their place of employment. Which leads them to go to a car dealership and search for a car and obtain a loan from a bank to finance the deal. The amount financed by the bank will depend on whether or not the person is capable of using some of their own money toward the purchase of the vehicle. This is how I have purchased the cars that I have had and currently own which is what most people do. Similarly when someone wants to purchase a home they search a particular area with the help of a realtor for a house that fits their needs and budget. After a property has been located the person approaches a bank hoping to secure a mortgage for their new home and if approved they move into the house. We must also look at student loans and with the cost of a college education going higher and higher it's no wonder that those who earn degrees are in so much debt that it will take them thirty years to repay. Parents are sending their children off to college with the hope that a degree will give the child a brighter financial future. Every parent wants their child to have a better life and higher education can certainly do that but it can also put the child debt for many years. I speak on this from my own experience because having gone to two different colleges in the 1980's to obtain my degrees it took me seventeen years to repay my student loan debt. During those seventeen years there were times where I was stressed out about having so much debt to repay. Along with the student loan debt I was just trying to make sure that I had the daily necessities of life. When I watch the news and I hear about a college increasing its tuition I feel bad for the students that are enrolled at the school because they will struggle with repaying their debt for longer than I did. Loans are a way to obtain certain things that we need in life but the borrower must be cautious because they may spend more years than they expected in repaying their financial obligations. Money that could have been used to invest and create a return for their retirement when they reach that age in life.

Credit cards are another form of a loan but with more freedom because you can take the card that has been issued by a bank and use it almost anywhere to purchase goods and services that you can pay some of or all of the amount at a later date. This is why many people have run into debt because they use credits cards without thinking about the consequences of over spending. Not only do people often overspend with regards to credit cards but most people never check to see what the interest rates are on the card and whether that rate is fixed or variable.

The interest rate is important to know because it also determines how much extra in finance charges you are paying each month for using the credit cards or for carrying over a balance from month to month. When you get your next credit card statement before you write the check for the minimum payment. Carefully go over your bill and look at the interest rate, the interest you were charged for the month and how long it will take to pay off the debt by making only minimum payments. Hopefully seeing this information in black and white will cause you to adjust how you use credit cards and even how you make your payments. Again I speak from personal experience because at one time I got a little out of hand with using a credit card. I learned from that experience and want others who choose to use credit cards to be wise and not to fall into the trap of overspending. When you excessively use your credit cards the bank loves you for it however, if you miss payments they will threaten or talk nasty to you because you are their slave. As I stated previously slaves are not treated with kindness and respect they are regarded as less than which has been seen throughout history. I want to encourage you to control your spending or use of credit cards so that you will limit how much of a slave you are to a bank or lending institution.

Now let me go back to the bible because God the Father does not want His people to be borrowers which is stated this way; *Deuteronomy 28:12 (KJV) The Lord shall open unto thee his good treasure, the heaven to give the rain unto thy land in his season, and to bless all the work of thine hand: and thou shalt lend unto many nations, and thou shalt not borrow.* God the Father spoke these words through Moses to the Israelites but they apply to believers today that they are not supposed to be slaves by borrowing. Please understand that as a Christian that God does not want you to be stressed because you have borrowed and cannot repay your financial obligations. The heavenly Father desires for you to be in a position where you can lend to others. Furthermore, when you do borrow God expects for you to make every effort to repay what you have borrowed; *Psalm 37:21 (KJV) The wicked borroweth, and payeth not again: but the righteous showeth mercy, and giveth.* Our heavenly Father looks at us as being wicked when we borrow and do not pay off our debts. If you were lending someone money you would want that person to keep their word and repay you your money. We must be the kind of people who are truthful and keep our promises to others because it pleases God. There may come a time in our lives where God tells us to borrow or to obtain a loan of some kind. This occurred when God the Father told the Israelites to borrow from their Egyptian neighbors and what God was doing was using the wealth of the Egyptians to finance the Israelites departure to a new land. I must stress the importance of or the fact that you must know God's voice and be certain that He has instructed you to borrow. Someone will read this and go and borrow or take out a loan on something that they want and then say that it is what God told them to. When they know that God never spoke to them about borrowing in the first place. You must know for sure that God has spoken to you about borrowing because when He instructs you to borrow then He will take responsibility for the repayment of the loan. Which is confirmed in scripture because God told the Israelites to borrow and later parted the Red Sea and destroyed the Egyptian Army cancelling the debt that was borrowed by the Israelites. The Israelites did not have to repay the loan that was borrowed because God not only told them to borrow but supernaturally wiped out the balance of the debt. He did not want His people to be financial slaves and set them free and our heavenly Father wants all His children to be financially free. There is nothing that is too hard or impossible for God to do and maybe there were among the people some who wondered how would the Egyptians be repaid. If there were any Israelites who pondered the wealth that was borrowed and its repayment those thoughts ended when Pharaoh's army drowned in the Red Sea. Had Pharaoh's army recaptured the Israelites then all of the wealth that had been borrowed would have been returned to its rightful owner. Let me go back to a story that I mentioned in a previous chapter about the widow woman who was told by Elisha to borrow as many pots as possible. Her sons were about to be made slaves because of their parents careless spending habits. The widow is scared but after Elisha gives her instructions she follows them and sells the oil that she has poured into the many pots that she has borrowed. God cancelled her debt because the heavenly Father does not want His people to live in debt but to live debt free.

I want to also mention about co-signing loans for other people because you may end up making the payments if the original borrower defaults. Often we are trying to help out a family member or close friend but we must be careful co-signing a loan because it could have disastrous consequences and possibly destroy a relationship. Personally I avoid co-signing loans for family and friends because I believe it makes my life easier by just saying no. Plenty of people have co-signed loans trying to help someone and ended up being used by the person and stuck with repaying a loan that they did not expect to have. Sometimes we may think that the person that has asked us for help is responsible but we may soon learn that they are irresponsible in the area of their finances. Many parents have co-signed loans for their children while sending them to college only to have that child either not finish school or finish and make no effort to repay the loan. Leaving the aging parents with the task of finding a way to repay a student loan. At a time when the parents should be using their money and wealth to build a nest egg for their golden years of retirement.

Another topic that I feel should be mentioned is bartering which allows someone to get what they need with what they already have. I had seen a television program on this some years ago where the people used bartering quite often but I never gave it much thought. Recently I was reading the bible when I came across a story on the subject of bartering that is found in 1 Kings 5 where Solomon and Hiram used this system. In this particular story Solomon who is the king of Israel has made plans for a temple to be built for people to gather to worship God. He needs building materials and sends a request to Hiram who is the king of Tyre for lumber because he has a great forest or supply of the trees that are needed for building the temple. These two kings come to an agreement where Hiram will supply Solomon with lumber in exchange for grain or wheat. Both men were able to get what they needed without using their money or wealth. Bartering might be something that more people should consider doing in an effort to obtain things that they need.

I hope that this chapter has caused you to take a closer look at your spending habits and to think about making any necessary changes. By you deciding to make and implement changes to your spending habits will over time greatly improve your finances. After all your goal should be to have more financial freedom and less debt which will allow you to accumulate more money and wealth for you and your family. God the Father speaks confirming how He desires for you to be free from debt but it is up to you to act upon and apply His instructions. As I close this chapter I thought it was important to end with a list of six things that I think every person should have which are:

1) Savings Account
2) Checking Account
3) Retirement Account
4) Life Insurance
5) Health Insurance
6) Last Will and Testament

Highlights/Notes

1. The borrower is a slave to the one who has the power to lend.

2. You must be careful taking out loans or using credit cards.

3. It could take longer than expected to pay off debts.

4. God told the Israelites to borrow and later cancelled their debt.

5. You must be responsible and payoff loans and other debts.

6. Bartering is a way to get things by using what you already have.

7. Bartering was used by Solomon and Hiram.

Conclusion

Writing a book of this magnitude on the topic of money and wealth would not have been possible for me twenty two years ago when I first entered the ministry. At that time I believed that God did not like for Christians to have money or to be wealthy. I believed that Jesus was poor and that the only thing that God wanted was for me to receive salvation and that I would receive money, wealth and everything else later when I got to heaven. There were many preachers that I heard back then that reinforced this type of thinking and I totally believed them. However, over the years I began to question some of the things that these preachers were saying so I started digging deeper into the bible for answers about money and wealth. As I studied more and more I began to realize that these preachers were wrong and eventually I heard preachers who were saying that there was nothing wrong with having money or wealth. Then the Holy Spirit opened my mind to a new level of greater understanding about money and wealth from the scriptures. Which has set me on a new path that has prepared me to faithfully believe that the promises of God in the bible can be mine so that I can live my best life. Things that I once thought were only available to a select few believers are also possible for me to fulfill in my lifetime. Now I see and understand that God does not have a problem with money or wealth and because of this new knowledge I was inspired to write this book. My desire is to help to break the poverty mentally that many believers have and see the chains of the spirit of poverty fall from their lives once and for all. Poverty is a spirit sent from the devil to keep the people of God from fulfilling their divine destiny and from being a powerful force in spreading the Gospel of Christ throughout the world. We the followers of Christ are meant to be leaders in the world so that the unsaved will receive Jesus as Lord and Savior then join us in claiming new territory for God. When the unsaved of this world constantly witness the members of God's kingdom always poor, broke and in lack. It makes it look as if God as a loving father does not take care of His children. With a deep desire to set the record straight on God's views on money and wealth I embarked on this journey hoping to reach those who want the rich promises of God to manifest in their lives. There will be those who will be critical of the words of this book and who will strongly disagree with what I have written. That is fine because everyone will not be open to change or to making a shift in a new direction where they can experience money and wealth from God. The examples that have been used in this book come from the bible and were people who experienced great levels of money and wealth. In each situation it was God who was the source or provider of that money and wealth. Our heavenly Father is the source who wants to give into the lives of His people but they must live for and serve Him with their whole heart. I hope and pray that those individuals who read this book and receive its contents will come away from the experience empowered to believe God for more and also be willing to share their good fortune with others. Sharing your money and wealth with others as God directs you to do so will have an impact on the lives of the recipients while bringing glory and magnifying the name of Almighty God. Money and wealth is neither good nor bad but how someone obtains it and how it is used can be good or bad. Hopefully the more God increases you in life the more things you will do for the kingdom, for you and your family and the world in which you live. Never let money or wealth control you but make sure that you always are in control of it. You are destined to do great and mighty things for God's kingdom and you need money and wealth to complete your assignment so stay the course and finish strong. Today begins a new day as you will have more than enough money and wealth to complete divine projects, live a more enjoyable financial life and leave an inheritance that will overflow for future generations.

www.ingramcontent.com/pod-product-compliance
Lightning Source LLC
Chambersburg PA
CBHW021503210526
45463CB00002B/865